Quick Quiz!

OPPOSITES

What is the missing letter?

EXAMPLE:

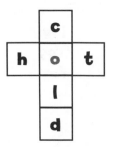

THE FIVE MINUTE TEST!

1

```
    b
    e
a t e r
    o
2   r
  h e
s   d
  p
  p
  y
```

3
```
    f
    u
p a s
    u
    r
    e
```

4
```
  h
e   s y
  r
  d
```

W9-CFK-273

Quick Quiz!

SHORT O

Use these **short O** words
to complete the story.

pond	log	hop
rock	frog	got
	fox	

THE FIVE MINUTE TEST!

The green _____ jumped

over a fallen _____. She saw a red

_____ hiding behind a large

_____. With one big _____,

she _____ safely

to the _____ .

Quick Quiz!

COMPOUND WORDS

Put two words together to make a new word. Draw lines to make new words. Write the new words on the lines.

cow	box
fire	bow
cup	cake
mail	fish
rain	boy
foot	ball
star	fly

THE FIVE MINUTE TEST!

_____

_____

_____

_____

_____

_____

_____

Answers: *Any order.* cowboy, firefly, cupcake, mailbox, rainbow, football, starfish

Quick Quiz!

Ant Riddles!

Match the description with each "ant" word.

A. tarantula
B. can't
C. National Anthem
D. pants

E. mantis
F. Santa Fe
G. Antarctica
H. g.i. ants

THE FIVE MINUTE TEST!

1. They're in the army. [ ]
2. They come in pairs. [ ]
3. It's hairy and scary. [ ]
4. Just an excuse! [ ]
5. It prays and preys! [ ]
6. It's patriotic. [ ]
7. Way down south. [ ]
8. It's in New Mexico. [ ]

Answers: 1. H 2. D 3. A 4. B 5. E 6. C 7. G 8. F

Quick Quiz!

LONG O

The letters **oa** can make the **long O sound.** Use these **long O** words to complete the story.

boat	**coat**	**toast**
float	**toad**	**oak**
goat	**coast**	**road**

THE FIVE MINUTE TEST!

A _____ wanted to

_____ in a _____ up the

_____. He met a _____

wearing a _____ hopping down the

_____. "Come to my house by the

_____ tree," he called, "and we will

have tea and _____!"

Answers: goat, float, boat, coast, toad, coat, road, oak, toast

Quick Quiz!

LONG A

Words with **ay** and **ai** can make the **long A sound.** Write long A words to answer the riddles.

hay	pail
tray	train
clay	tail
stay	paint
play	rain

THE FIVE MINUTE TEST!

1. I can carry food. _____

2. I am at the end of a dog. _____

3. I fall from the sky. _____

4. I ride on a track. _____

5. Farm animals eat me. _____

6. You can mold me. _____

7. I spruce up a wall. _____

8. I'm fun to do. _____

Answers: 1. pail/tray, 2. tail, 3. rain, 4. train, 5. hay, 6. clay, 7. paint, 8. play

Quick Quiz!

Good Job!

How many words can you think of that can also mean:

REALLY GOOD!

The Five Minute Test!

_____

_____ _____

_____ _____

_____ _____

_____ _____

_____

Possible Answers: great, awesome, fabulous, super, superb, fantastic, amazing, stupendous, excellent, tops, cool, wonderful, incredible, marvelous, terrific

©2021 Bendon

Quick Quiz!

©2021 Bendon

QUESTION WORDS

Write the words in alphabetical order.

when
which
what
why
who
how
where
whose

THE FIVE MINUTE TEST!

1. _____

2. _____

3. _____

4. _____

5. _____

6. _____

7. _____

8. _____

Answers: 1. how, 2. what, 3. when, 4. where, 5. which, 6. who, 7. whose, 8. why

Quick Quiz!

COMBINATION SOUNDS:
IR, ER, UR

Ir, er, and **ur** can
have the same sound.
Unscramble the words to write
ir, er, and **ur** words.

EXAMPLE:

nsrue = nurse

THE FIVE MINUTE TEST!

1. rdbi _____

2. hrsit _____

3. marfer _____

4. lirg _____

5. sruep _____

6. rtlteu _____

7. nidren _____

8. tfltyubre _____

9. wlfore _____

Answers: 1. bird, 2. shirt, 3. farmer, 4. girl, 5. purse, 6. turtle, 7. dinner, 8. butterfly, 9. flower

Quick Quiz!

Woo-Hoo!

Lots of words rhyme with **MOO**,
like dew, chew, grew, through, and gnu.
Can you find 17, too?

BLUE	DO	EWE	YEW	YOU	FLEW
FLUE	GLUE	GOO	HUE	HEW	NEW
SHOE	TO	TWO	WHO	ZOO	

Do you need a **CLUE?**
You will use every letter!

THE FIVE MINUTE TEST!

```
Z  B  F  L  U  E
O  G  L  U  E  S
O  H  E  U  H  W
G  T  W  O  E  E
D  O  E  Y  W  N
```

Quick Quiz!

A RHYME AROSE...

How many words do you
suppose your brain knows
that rhyme with:

ROSE

THE FIVE MINUTE TEST!

_____

_____   _____

_____   _____

_____   _____

_____   _____

_____   _____

_____

Quick Quiz!

BRAINSTORMING FUN!

Use your noodle to think up words in each category using the letters in:

GREAT

THE FIVE MINUTE TEST!

	Boy's Name	Girl's Name	A Food	An animal
G				
R				
E				
A				
T				

Quick Quiz!

CONTRACTIONS

Draw lines to match the words
and contractions. Use the contractions
to finish the story.

would not	**I've**
do not	**didn't**
did not	**that's**
I am	**wouldn't**
had not	**don't**
that is	**hadn't**
I have	**I'm**

THE FIVE MINUTE TEST!

"I _____ do that if I were you,"

warned Mom. She knew I _____ have time

to play outside because I _____ finished my

homework. "_____ planning on finishing my

homework when it gets dark," I said. "I _____

have much left to do."   "_____ not the

first time _____ heard that

excuse," said Mom.

Quick Quiz!

Long I

Sometimes **y**, **ie**, and **igh** make the **long I sound.** Add and subtract letters to write **long I** words.

Example:

th + ry – h = try

The Five Minute Test!

1. w + sh – s + y = _____

2. ch + re – he + y = _____

3. p + li + ed – ld = _____

4. t + ib + he – bh = _____

5. li + gr + ht – r = _____

6. n + igh + wt – w = _____

7. hi + gs + h – s = _____

8. me + yes – ee + elf = _____

Quick Quiz!

GET INTO THE GROOVE!

How many words can you
make using the letters in:

SHAKE, RATTLE, AND ROLL

THE FIVE MINUTE TEST!

Quick Quiz!

SCORE!

Many words rhyme with **SCORE**, like oar, tore, chore, poor, your, and store. How many more can you find in 5 minutes?

BOAR	CORE	DOOR	DRAWER	FLOOR
FOUR	NOR	OR	ORE	PORE
POUR	ROAR	SHORE	SNORE	SOAR
WAR	WORE			

THE FIVE MINUTE TEST!

Hint: Every letter is used at least once.

what's your score?

```
B  O  A  R     C  D
O  R  A  O  R  E
S  W  R  A  O  S
N  E  W  O  R  E
O  E  R  U  O  P
R  O  O  D  N  O
E  F  L  O  O  R
   S  H  O  R  E
```

Quick Quiz!

R Blends

Add and subtract letters
to write words with an **r blend**.

Example:

br + oe – e + om = broom

The Five Minute Test!

1. br + iou – io + sh = _____

2. cr + oew – e + n = _____

3. fr + suits – ss = _____

4. dr + iue + m – ie = _____

5. pr + ee + tty – e = _____

6. cr + aeo + b – eo = _____

7. t + raise + n – se = _____

8. gr + howl – h – l = _____

Quick Quiz!

HUE ARE AMAZING!

How many color words
can you think of besides
red, blue, and **yellow?**

THE FIVE MINUTE TEST!

_____

_____   _____

_____   _____

_____   _____

_____   _____

_____   _____

_____

Possible Answers: green, purple, orange, pink, black, white, gray, brown, tan, teal, aqua, peach, maroon, lime, violet, silver, gold, lavender, cream, rose, olive

Quick Quiz!

SCRAMBLED EGGS

Can you unscramble all these "egg" words in only **5 minutes?**

EXAMPLE:

ethwi = white

THE FIVE MINUTE TEST!

1. ehiccnk _____

2. drib _____

3. crotan _____

4. hisf _____

5. slleh _____

6. petrile _____

7. kreab _____

8. loky _____

9. nozed _____

10. drefid _____

11. diary _____

12. stabek

Answers: 1. chicken, 2. bird 3. carton, 4. fish, 5. shell, 6. reptile, 7. break, 8. yolk, 9. dozen, 10. fried, 11. dairy, 12. basket

Quick Quiz!

SAME SOUND

Think of a word that sounds
the same as each word, but
is spelled a different way.

Example: blue blew

1. hear
2. prince
3. paws
4. sent

5. wheel
6. daze
7. clothes
8. some

9. choose
10. guest
11. our
12. nose

THE FIVE MINUTE TEST!

1. _____

2. _____

3. _____

4. _____

5. _____

6. _____

7. _____

8. _____

9. _____

10. _____

11. _____

12. _____

Quick Quiz!

WORDS ARE FUN!

How many words can you make
in 5 minutes using the letters in:

STAR STUDENT

Letters may be used more than once.

THE FIVE MINUTE TEST!

_____

_____   _____

_____   _____

_____   _____

_____   _____

_____   _____

_____

Quick Quiz!

©2021 Bendon

ST, SP, AND SN BLENDS

Add and subtract letters to write **st**, **sp**, and **sn** words.

EXAMPLE:

st + amy + p − y = stamp

THE FIVE MINUTE TEST!

1. sp + loo − l + n = _____

2. sn + ack + e − c = _____

3. sn + aie + l − e = _____

4. s + ta + dr − d = _____

5. s + pid + ler − l = _____

6. sne − e + a + ck = _____

7. s + true + amp − are = _____

8. sp + o + tch − ch = _____

Answers: 1. spoon, 2. snake, 3. snail, 4. star, 5. spider, 6. snack, 7. stump, 8. spot

Quick Quiz!

Dino Word Dig!

Can you find all these
dinosaur words in 5 minutes?

DIG	EGGS	PLATES	SPIKE	REPTILE
TEETH	EXTINCT	TONS	T-REX	BONES
CLAWS	HUGE	TAIL	DINOSAURS	OLD

THE FIVE MINUTE TEST!

```
D Z M T O N S T E
P I T E E T H K X
L R N O L D I E T
A S G O F P R H I
T E G G S T R Y N
E I J C L A W S C
S E G U H I U W T
R E P T I L E R B
G I D H B O N E S
```

Quick Quiz!

WHAT DO YOU SEE?

Study the scene. Can you spot
objects that rhyme with...

FLAT	FREE	HOOT
____	____	____
____	____	____
____	____	____
____	____	____

THE FIVE MINUTE TEST!

Possible Answers: hat, cat, mat, bat, slat; tree, ski, three, key, knee; boot, flute, suit, fruit, root, newt